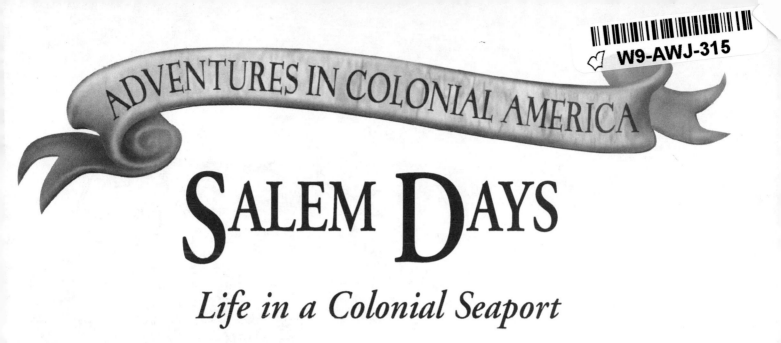

ADVENTURES IN COLONIAL AMERICA

SALEM DAYS

Life in a Colonial Seaport

by James E. Knight

illustrated by David Wenzel

Troll

Cover art by Shi Chen.

Library of Congress Cataloging-in-Publication Data

Knight, James E.
    Salem days.

    Summary: A young farm boy running away to sea in
1774 explores the Salem harbor while waiting for his
ship to sail.
    1. Salem (Mass.)—Social life and customs—Juvenile
literature.   2. Salem (Mass.)—Harbor—Juvenile literature.   3. Salem (Mass.)—Commerce—Juvenile literature.
4. Shipping—Massachusetts—Salem—Juvenile literature.
[1. Salem (Mass.)—History.   2. Shipping—Massachusetts
—Salem.   3. Seafaring life.   4. United States—History
—Colonial period, ca. 1600–1775]   I. Wenzel, David,
1950–   ill.   II. Title.
F74.S1K64   974.4'5   81-23076
ISBN 0-89375-732-2 (lib. bdg.)   AACR2
ISBN 0-8167-4803-9 (pbk.)

This edition published 1998 by Troll Communications L.L.C.

Printed in the United States of America.

10   9   8   7   6   5   4   3   2

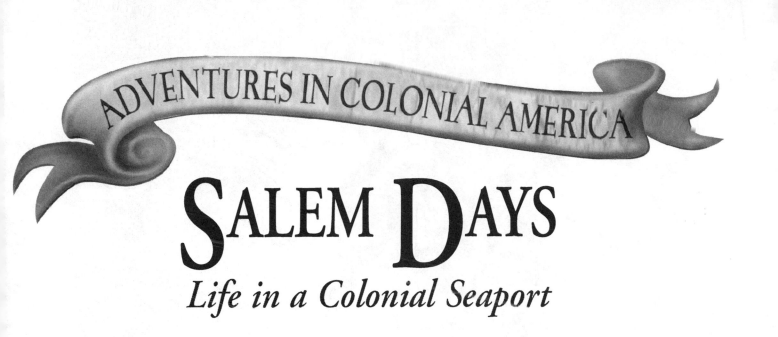

ADVENTURES IN COLONIAL AMERICA

SALEM DAYS

Life in a Colonial Seaport

Young Joshua Silsbee stood on a rocky hill above Salem, Massachusetts. The year was 1774. In the early light of the October morning, he could see the deep blue of the harbor before him. Geese honked overhead, as a light breeze rippled the surface of the water. The pale rays of the sun caught the masts of dozens of ships at anchor. Here and there, Josh could see a sail being hoisted.

Joshua Silsbee was fifteen years old, alone, scared, and already homesick. For, like so many other Yankee farm boys, he had decided to run away to sea. Josh had heard sailors tell of great adventure in the West Indies, and of the money to be made at the end of a sea voyage. His own cousin had spent three years at sea. He had returned with enough money to buy a farm and get married.

Far behind Josh was his father's farm, but he would not look back. He ran his fingers through his straw-colored hair and thought of the note he had left for his mother. She would be upset when she read it this morning. Last night he had packed his few belongings and left. In the note, he told his mother that he was unhappy with the life and work of the farm. Milking cows and digging up tree stumps were not for him.

Now he was afraid of what lay ahead. He could still turn back. It wasn't too late. If he ran right home, he could tear up the note before his mother found it. But if he started down the hill toward Salem, Josh knew there would be no turning back.

He took a deep breath, squared his shoulders, and began to walk down the hill toward the harbor. By the time he reached the streets of Salem, his fears were behind him. He was caught up in the bustling business of the city and the tingling smells of the waterfront.

There were many ships anchored at Crowinshield's Wharf. But Josh looked for only one. There it lay—the brig *Salem's Pride*. A friend had told Josh that the ship needed a crew for the next voyage. They would take a "green hand" like himself—someone who had never been to sea before.

As Josh climbed the steep gangplank of the *Salem's Pride*, the smells of the harbor filled his nostrils—salt water and rope and tea and spices. He liked the smells, and the bustle of people going places.

At the top of the gangplank, Josh asked to come aboard. A petty officer motioned him forward. The officer was deeply tanned. His hair was tied in a pigtail at the back of his neck.

Josh could hardly believe it was this easy. In less than ten minutes, he had signed his name to the ship's papers. Joshua Silsbee was now a part of the crew of the *Salem's Pride.*

A seaman led Josh below to the forecastle, where the crew slept. A boy, about the same age as Josh, was there. He pointed out Josh's bunk. Josh put down his small bag of belongings on the bed. Inside the bag, he carried six large New England cheeses. He planned to sell them in a foreign port, or trade them for spices, such as pepper and cinnamon. Josh had been told that each sailor was given space on the ship to carry his own trading goods.

The young man, whose name was Silas, shook hands with Josh. "Might as well get acquainted," he said with a smile. "We're going to be shipmates for the next four years."

Silas had run away from a farm, too, near Marblehead, a few miles down the coast. Boys of fourteen to
sixteen years old often left their homes for the magic of the
sea. They signed up as crew members on ships from places
like Mystic, Cohasset, Newburyport, and New Bedford.

Besides the lure of the sea, there was the thrill of traveling to foreign places. The pay was good, too—much better than English seamen got. In 1774, boys of Josh's age were paid from six to eight dollars a month by Salem ship owners. That was much more than they could earn on the farm. Most of these young seamen planned to return home one day and buy land. But for now, the life of a sailor seemed full of excitement.

What Josh and Silas did not know yet was how hard and how dangerous a sailor's life was. Many a young man never returned home. Some Yankee trading ships disappeared at sea and were never heard of again. Some went down in terrible storms in the West Indies or off the African coast. Some seamen died in battles with Barbary pirates in the Mediterranean or with Indians in Venezuela. And if they survived that, many were killed by disease— scurvy, typhus, or the dreaded yellow jack.

But for those who were daring, hard working, smart, and lucky, there was money to be made as a sailor. And if a seaman made captain, he would be wealthy indeed. Some Yankee seamen became ship captains by the time

Rope and Lead Weight
Used to Measure Water's Depth

they were twenty years old. They received up to eight percent of the profits from each voyage, besides their pay. And they could take five tons of goods of their own to trade in foreign ports. That would bring in a lot more than Josh's six cheeses! It was no wonder that many young sea captains left the sea and set themselves up in business by the time they had reached the age of thirty.

Josh and Silas could hardly wait for the voyage to begin. But the captain of the *Salem's Pride* had found some rotten planks near the water line. They had to be replaced. So the ship was towed to the shipyard for repair work. It would be two weeks before the voyage began.

But there was much to see and do in those two weeks. The boys had work to do aboard the ship. When that was done, they were allowed to explore the city of Salem.

Josh and Silas spent hours walking about the streets, the wharves, and the shipyard. They liked the smells of the pitch and tar that were used to stop leaks in the ships. They liked to walk on the thick bed of wood chips and shavings that carpeted the shipyard.

One day they watched a new ship being launched.

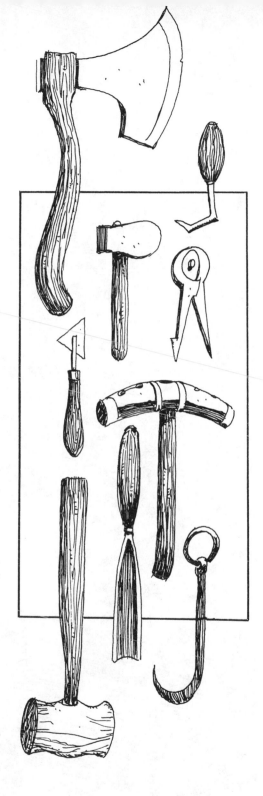

First, they listened to speeches by some of the ship's owners. A band played. Then several men knocked out the timbers that propped up the new ship's hull. The crowd cheered as the *Lydia Parsons* began to slide down the wooden tracks. Faster and faster, it slid, until the stern entered the blue harbor in a shower of spray.

Josh and Silas wandered through every neighborhood in Salem. The only place Josh wouldn't go was the busy farmer's market on South Street. He knew his father often sold vegetables at the market, and Josh did not want to risk meeting him. His father would haul him right back to the farm if he caught him—and probably give him a caning with a hickory stick besides.

Josh and Silas met a lot of fishermen in Salem, many of them boys about their own age. Fishing for cod was a big industry in colonial New England. Thousands of tons of dried and salted codfish were shipped each year from the shores of New England to Spain, France, and the West Indies.

Unlike the long voyage Josh and Silas were to take, the cod fishermen were at sea for only a few weeks at a time.

They could make three or four trips a year and live at home with their families the rest of the time.

Some of the owners of cod schooners had grown very wealthy. When one of the ships came in loaded with cod, the owner received almost half the profits as his share. The rest was divided among the crew.

Josh and Silas boarded a cod schooner one day. The air was strong with the smell of fish. They watched as the sailors dried hundreds of salted cod on the deck in the heat of the blazing sun.

Another day Josh was sent on an errand to Peabody's Countinghouse. He was to deliver a small, brassbound box to Hamilton Shay, the chief clerk. Mr. Shay would give him a written receipt for the package.

In 1774, a colonial countinghouse was a very busy and important place. It was a bank, an insurance company, an employment office, a business office, and a stock market. It was in the countinghouse that shares in ships' profits were bought and sold, and money was lent to outfit ships. Gold was weighed on scales, officers were hired by ship owners, and cash was kept in vaults.

While Josh was waiting in the bustling countinghouse for his receipt, he could look right into the office of Mr. Peabody himself. On the office door was his name—printed in big letters. Outside the office were the clerks—boys about Josh's own age. Seated on high stools, they were all busily writing in large ledger books.

Josh was glad to leave the countinghouse, when the receipt was ready. He thought working there must be about as dull as working on the farm.

But Josh didn't think it dull the next day, when he delivered a message to someone on Chestnut Street. This was the finest street in Salem, where many wealthy people lived in their beautiful homes. The first mate of the *Salem's Pride* sent Josh with a note for one of the ship's owners, Elijah Dobbs.

Josh waited in the hall for a reply to the message. He could see into the huge parlor. Everywhere were reminders of the sea, for Mr. Dobbs had been a sailor in his younger years. Josh could see a high, carved mantelpiece, with columns on each side. A fine clock chimed the hour. Carvings of anchors and eagles hung over the doorways.

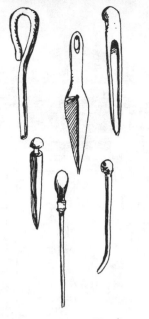

Sailmaker's Tools

When Josh left Mr. Dobbs' home on Chestnut Street, he thought it would be splendid if one day he could own a home there. And then he smiled at himself for having such a far-fetched dream.

On the way back to the ship, Josh headed for Carter's Ropewalk to get as much hemp line as he could carry. A ropewalk was a place where rope for ships was made. Every New England seaport town had at least one ropewalk.

As he passed Mallory's Sail Loft, Josh could see sailmakers using chalk to sketch the patterns for the sails. They spread large pieces of canvas on the floor of the loft and then cut out the sails. Josh watched the workers stitching rope onto the edges of some finished sails. As in most sail lofts, a potbellied stove hung from the ceiling. This saved floor space and gave the sailmakers a larger work area.

18

A little past the sail loft, Josh stopped to look at one of the most interesting places in any seaport town—the ship chandlery. Long before he reached the building, he could smell the sharp but pleasant odor of oakum, the stringy material used for filling the boat seams. A dozen clerks bustled about the chandlery, for here a customer could buy just about anything and everything needed on a ship.

Customers going on long voyages bought provisions, such as dried fish, salted meat, potatoes, flour, biscuits, and spices. The chandlery also sold anchors, lanterns, compasses, and a hundred other items.

When Josh left the chandlery, it wasn't hard to find the ropewalk. Except for the dock warehouses, it was the longest building in town. It had to be, for inside, hundreds of feet of rope were laid out. Josh could smell the hot pine tar that was used to soak the new rope to give it strength.

After he had placed his order, Josh watched the rope-makers at work. They formed the rope by first pulling the hemp fibers through long iron spikes to straighten them. Then a "spinner" tied the fibers around his waist and began to walk backward—the whole length of the building. As he walked, he braided the fibers into a thin rope called "yarn." At the far end of the shed, a boy turned a wheel that twisted the yarn as the spinner braided it. Three or more of the yarns would later be twisted together to make the finished rope.

When Josh returned to the ship, he learned that the *Salem's Pride* would be ready to sail in two days. On the day before they left, Josh and Silas took a final walk around the town. With his last English half-penny, Josh bought some fried fish and roasted chestnuts. He and Silas ate as they walked over to Crowinshield's Wharf.

At the dock, a small whaling ship was being unloaded. Longshoremen sweated as they rolled barrels of whale oil down the gangplank and into a long shed. From here it would be shipped to markets in England, France, and Spain. The whale oil would be used to light people's homes. A good number of Yankee whalers sailed out of Salem, but most of them sailed out of Nantucket, New Bedford, and Fairhaven.

23

Josh could see a tall Indian gazing down at them from the whaler's deck. His arms were folded across his bare chest. He wore a black hat with a wide brim, and two feathers hung behind his left ear.

"He's our best harpooner," said the whaler's cabin boy, who was standing on the wharf next to Josh and Silas. "He hails from Gay Head on Nantucket."

Josh nodded. Everyone knew that the Gay Head Indians were the best harpooners in the whaling trade.

The cabin boy, who looked no more than twelve years old, told Josh and Silas that the voyage had been a good one. They had spent over two and a half years at sea. Enough whales had been killed to barrel one hundred tons of whale oil. The oil was made by cooking strips of whale blubber. The blubber was cooked on deck over a brick oven called the "try-works."

"Maybe we should have signed on a whaling ship," said Silas to the cabin boy. "Is your pay good?"

The cabin boy shrugged. "Whalers aren't paid wages," he said. "Each man gets a share of the profits. The captain gets 1/18 of the profits, and an able seaman gets 1/75. But my share is the lowest. I get 1/120."

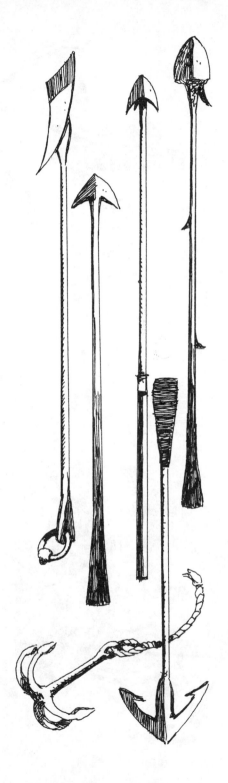

"I guess we'd better stay where we are," said Josh.

The next morning the *Salem's Pride* weighed anchor at last, and sailed on the outgoing tide. The sailors sang sea chanties as they walked around and around, turning the capstan—the machine that raised the heavy anchor rope.

Josh did not see Salem harbor again for forty-four months. During that time, he had many adventures. The *Salem's Pride* sailed down to South America, then to the Ivory Coast of Africa. Heading north, the ship passed Gibraltar and sailed into the Mediterranean Sea. There they stopped at many ports, trading in each one.

One day, while anchored near the Algerian coast, misfortune befell the *Salem's Pride*. A boatload of men had rowed ashore to get fresh water. As they were rowing back, a swift Barbary pirate ship appeared around a point of land and cut them off. The sailors were taken prisoners, and they were never found. Young Silas was among them. Josh was greatly saddened to lose his friend.

26

Now the *Salem's Pride* was badly short of men. The first mate had taken a liking to Josh and thought he was a good worker. Josh was willing to learn, and in his spare time, he studied the navigation books. The first mate promoted Josh to able seaman.

The *Salem's Pride* finally dropped anchor in Salem in 1777. Josh was now a boatswain's mate. When the crew of the ship had been paid at Peabody's Countinghouse, Josh walked away with eight hundred dollars in his pocket.

Josh began the long walk home. Along the way he saw people he knew, but no one recognized him. Taller and stronger, his face tanned a deep bronze, Joshua Silsbee was now nearly twenty years old.

There was great joy on the Silsbee farm when Josh returned. His father even forgave him for running away. Much had changed while the boy had been gone. For one thing, the Colonies were now at war with England. Many of the men from the port towns were going to sea, to fight the English in large ships called privateers. Josh decided to sign aboard a privateer himself.

When Josh shipped out a few weeks later on the privateer *Jacob Jonas*, he was on his way to a long and successful career.

By the time the war ended, Josh was the captain and part-owner of his ship. Salem now had more than one hundred and fifty privateers. These vessels were too large to be used as trade ships in the West Indies, even if the British would have allowed it. So the ships from Salem began to sail around the tip of Africa to such places as India, China, and the East Indies. This was the beginning of the wealthy China Trade period, which would last for the next fifty years. And Salem was at the heart of it.

The captains of many ships made their fortunes during this period. Joshua Silsbee was one of them. At the age of thirty-one, he retired from the sea and became a merchant.

In 1790, Josh married black-haired Mercy Gannett from Marblehead. A few months later, Josh and Mercy moved into a small but elegant house, set well back from the trees lining Chestnut Street.

30

Index

*(Page numbers that appear in **boldface** type refer to illustrations.)*

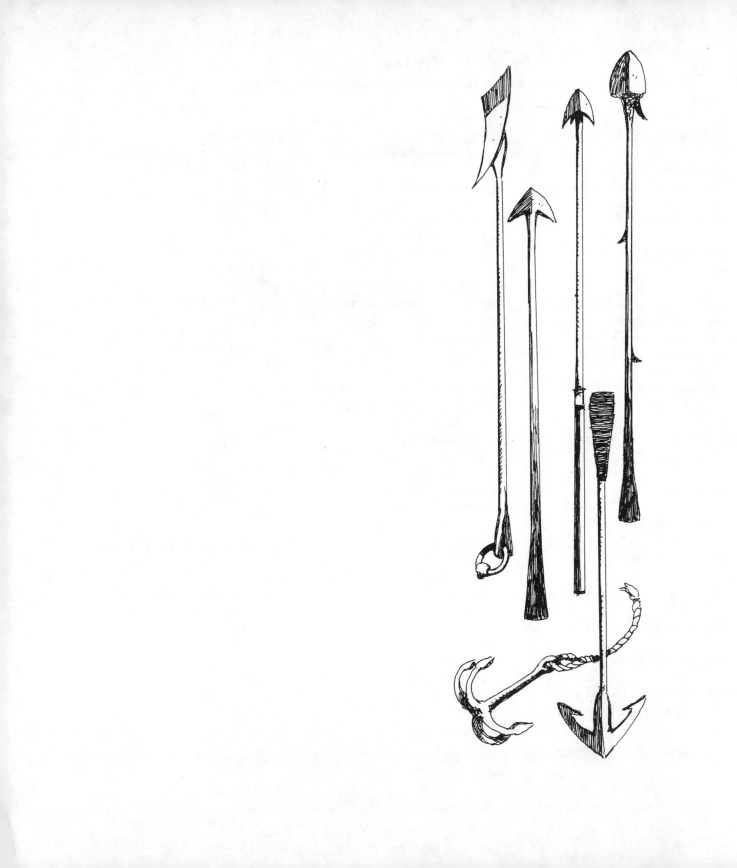